Reading for Comprehension
READINESS

Book 3

Written by Arlene Capriola and Rigmor Swensen
Illustrated by Laurie Conley

ISBN 978-0-8454-3857-2

Copyright © 2007 The Continental Press, Inc.

No part of this publication may be reproduced in any form or by any means, electronic, mechanical, photocopying, recording, or otherwise, without the prior written permission of the publisher. All rights reserved. Printed in the United States of America.

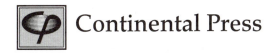

What do goats give us?

Have you ever seen a goat?
Some farmers raise goats.

Goats are smaller than cows.
But they give milk like cows.
People drink goat's milk.
They make cheese from it, too.

Goats are smaller than sheep.
But they have wool like sheep.
People make sweaters from it.
The sweaters are very warm.

Circle the letter for the right answer.

1. The story is about _____.

   a cows   b goats   c sheep

2. Some goats live _____.

   a on farms   b in houses   c in rivers

3. Goats are NOT as _____ as cows.

   a nice   b small   c big

4. You can tell from the story that cheese is made from _____.

   a wool   b milk   c grass

Write two words to finish the sentence.

Goats give us _____ and _____.

What animal looks like a log?

The alligator lives by the water.
It is very big.
This animal can swim all day.
It must have fish to eat.

The alligator slides into the water.
It is very still.
You can not see it move.

Fish swim by.
The animal looks like a log to the fish.
Soon the alligator will have dinner.

Circle the letter for the right answer.

1. This story tells about an animal that looks like a _____.

    a log   b rock   c fish

2. This animal lives _____.

    a in the desert   b on a log
              c near the water

3. The story says that the alligator can _____ all day.

    a move   b slide   c swim

4. You can tell that the alligator's dinner will be _____.

    a fish   b logs   c water

Write a word to finish the sentence.

You can not see an alligator _____.

How do horses sleep?

Many horses sleep standing up.
They do not fall over.
Why do horses do this?

Most horses do not go into a deep sleep.
They can come out of their sleep fast.

Horses have strong bones in their legs and feet.
They can run fast if there is trouble.
Because they sleep standing up,
horses are always ready to run.

Circle the letter for the right answer.

1. This story tells MOSTLY about how horses
   _____.

   a eat   b run   c sleep

2. Most horses are _____.

   a fast   b little   c brown

3. Horses are good runners because they have _____.

   a short legs   b strong bones   c big feet

4. You can tell that it takes _____ for a horse to wake up from a deep sleep.

   a more time   b not much time
               c ten minutes

Write two words to finish the sentence.

Horses sleep _____ _____.

What is a sea horse?

The sea horse looks like a horse.
But it does not have legs.
The sea horse is a fish.

This is a funny fish.
It looks like it is standing up when it swims.
It can look up and down at the same time.
It can change from brown to yellow to green.

The mother sea horse does not have the baby.
The father sea horse does!

Circle the letter for the right answer.

1. This story is about a _____.

    a fish   b horse   c father

2. The sea horse can change _____.

    a names   b colors   c legs

3. The _____ sea horse has the baby.

    a father   b mother   c sister

4. You can tell that the sea horse got its name because it _____ a horse.

    a is not   b is as big as   c looks like

Write two words to finish the sentence.

A sea horse can look _____ and _____ at the same time.

Do people live on Mars?

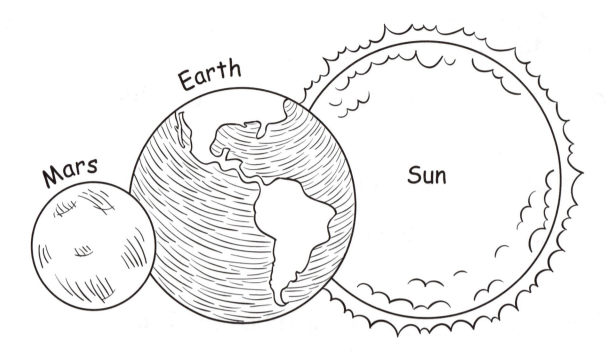

Earth is a planet.
Mars is a planet, too.
We can see it in the night sky.
It looks like a red star.

Does anyone live on Mars?
Once people said yes.
Today we know that they can not.
It is too cold there.

Some astronauts want to go to Mars.
But it is too far away.
Some day they may find a way.

Circle the letter for the right answer.

1. This story is about a _____.

    a country   b city   c planet

2. Mars looks like a _____ in the sky.

    a star   b ball   c sun

3. Mars looks small in the sky because it is _____.

    a a tiny star   b a new planet   c very far away

4. We can not see Mars _____.

    a at night   b in the day   c when it is cold

Write two words to finish the sentence.

_____ and _____ are both planets.

Who is Neil Armstrong?

People can walk on the moon.
Neil Armstrong was the first.
On Earth, people could see him on TV.
It was 1969.

Neil put his foot on the moon.
He said, "This is one small step for a man."
Then he walked on the moon.

Neil came back to Earth.
He told us many things.
He had moon rocks to show, too.

Circle the letter for the right answer.

1. This is a story about _____ on the moon.

   a TV   b a man   c a flag

2. Neil put his _____ on the moon.

   a bags   b name   c foot

3. _____ walked on the moon before Neil.

   a No one   b One man   c Many people

4. Because Neil went to the moon, _____.

   a everyone can go   b we can see it
        c we know more about it

Write a word to finish the sentence.

Neil was the _____ man on the moon.

Are there flowers in the desert?

The desert is very hot and dry.
It has a lot of sand.
Sometimes it has hills and rocks, too.

It does not rain much in the desert.
But the desert is very pretty after it rains.
Flowers come out very fast.
They last for just one or two days.
Then they go away.
You must wait for the next rain.
Then there will be flowers again.

Circle the letter for the right answer.

1. This story tells about a _____.

    a place   **b** flower   **c** rock

2. The desert is NOT _____.

    a dry   **b** wet   **c** hot

3. Flowers make the desert look _____.

    a hot   **b** wet   **c** pretty

4. You can tell that flowers need _____ to come out.

    a rain   **b** snow   **c** wind

Write a word to finish the sentence.

You can see _____ in the dry desert.

What is karate?

Did you ever do karate?
Many girls and boys do.
They go to a class for karate.
They learn ways to be safe.

In karate class, you think a lot.
First you learn to bow.
Then you learn more karate.
You learn to do the karate kick.

One day, you get a white karate belt.
You learn more karate.
After a long time, you may get a black belt.

Circle the letter for the right answer.

1. This story is all about _____.

   a skating   b football   c karate

2. You can learn karate in a _____.

   a show   b class   c movie

3. In karate you learn to _____ first.

   a kick   b move   c bow

4. You can tell from the story that you _____ to do karate.

   a stand up   b sit down   c lie on the floor

Write two words to finish the sentence.

You must work to get a _____ _____ in karate.

What could dinosaurs do?

Dinosaurs lived a long time ago.
Some dinosaurs were very small.
Others were very, very big.

Some dinosaurs had long, sharp teeth.
They ate other animals.
But some big dinosaurs just ate plants.

Some dinosaurs could walk on two legs.
Some could swim in the sea.
Other dinosaurs could fly.

There are no dinosaurs today.
But there are dinosaur bones.
That is how we know about them.

Circle the letter for the right answer.

1. This story tells about an animal _____.

   a with no tail   b from long ago   c on TV

2. There were NO dinosaurs that could _____.

   a swim   b talk   c fly

3. Dinosaur bones tell us that dinosaurs _____.

   a were real   b are still alive   c were made up

4. You can tell that dinosaurs did NOT need _____ to eat plants.

   a strong bones   b big wings
            c sharp teeth

Write two words to finish the sentence.

Some dinosaurs were very _____, and some were very _____.

What is in a rain forest?

A rain forest is a special place.
It is hot. It rains a lot, too.
So, plants can grow fast.

In a rain forest it is dark and still.
There are tall trees.
They look like they reach the sky.
They have very big leaves.

Many kinds of animals live in a rain forest.
Lemurs can jump from branch to branch.
Beautiful birds live in the trees.
Some people live in the rain forest, too.

Circle the letter for the right answer.

1. This story is MOSTLY about a special _____.

    a animal   b bird   c place

2. _____ people live in the rain forest.

    a No   b Some   c Small

3. In this story the word <u>still</u> means _____.

    a yet   b quiet   c dark

4. You can tell from the story that <u>lemurs</u> are _____.

    a animals   b birds   c fish

Write two words to finish the sentence.

_____ and _____ live in the rain forest.

Why do we call some people Indians?

Christopher Columbus wanted to go to India.
But he sailed the wrong way.
He came to America instead.
He did not know it was America.

Other people lived here.
They lived in teepees and long log houses.

Columbus said, "This is India."
So he called the people Indians.
But they were not Indians.
Today we call them American Indians.

Circle the letter for the right answer.

1. This story tells about the name we gave to some _____.

   a people   b animals   c lands

2. Columbus wanted to go to _____.

   a Mars   b America   c India

3. In this story a teepee is a kind of _____.

   a ship   b house   c food

4. You can tell from the story that Columbus had to cross the _____.

   a sea   b river   c land

Write a word to finish the sentence.

Columbus called the people _____.

Where does the space shuttle go?

The space shuttle is like a rocket.
It goes into space.
Then it goes around the Earth.
Astronauts ride inside the shuttle.

The astronauts work and sleep there.
When they look down, they see a big blue ball.
That is the Earth.
They can look out into space, too.
That is how they learn about the moon and stars.

Then the space shuttle comes back to the Earth.
It lands just like an airplane.
Soon it will be ready for another trip.

Circle the letter for the right answer.

1. This story tells about something that _____.

   a runs   b flies   c hops

2. From space the Earth looks _____.

   a blue   b yellow   c green

3. Astronauts go into space to _____.

   a sleep   b learn   c talk

4. The space shuttle is MOST like an airplane when it _____.

   a goes up   b stays in space   c comes back

Write two words to finish the sentence.

The space shuttle flies around _____ _____.

What is a ghost town?

There are ghost towns in the West.
A ghost town does not have ghosts.
It does not have any people now.

At one time many people went to the West.
They went to find gold.
They lived in towns.
Most of them did not find gold.
So they left the towns.

Today we can visit the towns.
We can see the shops and houses.
But no one is in them.
So we say they are "ghost towns."

Circle the letter for the right answer.

1. This story is MOSTLY about old _____.

    a towns   b people   c farms

2. At one time many people went to the _____.

    a North   b East   c West

3. The people wanted to find _____.

    a homes   b gold   c jobs

4. You can tell that there was _____ gold in the West.

    a no   b some   c much

Write two words to finish the sentence.

No one lives in a _____ _____ .

How did Abe Lincoln learn to read?

Abe Lincoln was born about 200 years ago.
His mother died when he was a boy.
Abe wanted to learn many things.
He went to school for a short time.
Then he had to work.

But Abe learned to read.
His new mother helped him.
She had books for him.
There were no lamps.
Abe had to sit by the fire to read.

Abe learned a lot by reading.
He became a lawyer.
Then he became president of the U.S.

Circle the letter for the right answer.

1. This story is about a _____.

   a mother   b teacher   c president

2. Abe had to _____ to help his family.

   a go to school   b go to work
   c read books

3. Abe learned to read from his _____.

   a lawyer   b father   c new mother

4. You can tell from the story that Abe Lincoln's father _____.

   a got married again   b was a lawyer
   c liked to read

Write a word to finish the sentence.

Abe Lincoln became _____.

What is the Grand Canyon?

The Grand Canyon is a very big, deep hole.
It goes down into the earth.
The sides of the Grand Canyon are rock.
There is a river at the bottom.

Many people come to see the Grand Canyon.
You can hike down the sides.
Or you can ride down on a mule.
At the bottom there is a long bridge over the river.

Some people set up tents and camp there.
You can swim and fish in the river.
There is even a train to take you around.

Circle the letter for the right answer.

1. This story is MOSTLY about a _____.

   a long river   b place to fish

   c hole in the earth

2. The sides of the Grand Canyon are _____.

   a rock   b brick   c dirt

3. You can ride around the bottom of the Grand Canyon inside a _____.

   a train   b car   c mule

4. You can tell from this story that a <u>canyon</u> is probably a _____.

   a river   b hole   c rock

Write a word to finish the sentence.

You can _____ in the Grand Canyon.

What do sled dogs do?

Some dogs live in a cold place.
They have a lot of fur.
It keeps them warm.

These dogs can pull big sleds.
They are called sled dogs.
They are very strong.
Many dogs pull together.
The dogs run on top of the snow.

Every year there is a sled dog race.
The dogs work hard.
The race lasts for many days.
Which dog team will be the best?

Circle the letter for the right answer.

1. This story tells about a kind of _____.

   a dog   b sled   c snow

2. There are many dogs in a _____.

   a team   b sled   c house

3. A word that means "not cold" is _____.

   a ice   b fur   c warm

4. You can tell from the story that the dogs must _____.

   a sleep a lot   b work together
                   c eat snow

Write two words to finish the sentence.

A sled dog's _____ keeps it _____.

Go To Writing Page 47

Where is Antarctica?

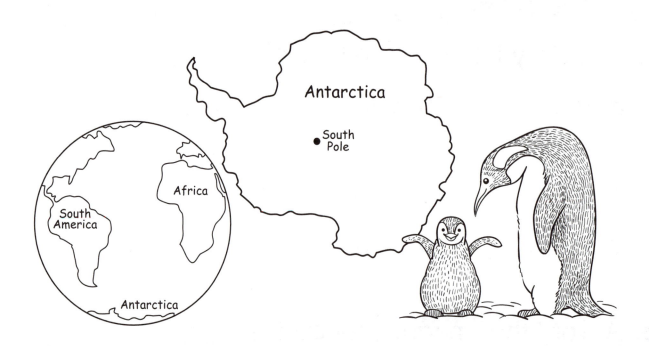

The land at the South Pole is called Antarctica.
It is very, very cold and windy there.
The snow does not melt.
It turns to ice when it falls.

In the winter it is dark all day.
The sun comes back in summer.
But it is still cold.

People do not live on Antarctica.
But some people go there to learn.
They study the penguins and seals that live there.
They learn about the ice, wind, and sun.

Circle the letter for the right answer.

1. This story is about a place that has lots of _____.

    a rain	b ice	c plants

2. In the winter, you can not see the _____.

    a snow	b seals	c sun

3. Some _____ live on Antarctica.

    a animals	b people	c plants

4. You can tell from the story that it is never _____ in Antarctica.

    a sunny	b warm	c windy

Write a word to finish the sentence.

The snow does not _____ in Antarctica.

Why is Oprah Winfrey special?

Oprah Winfrey has a show on TV.
She talks to people and makes them smile.
She has been in movies, too.
Oprah has a book club for kids.
And she has a magazine.

Oprah has worked hard.
Now she is very rich.
What does Oprah do with her money?
She gives lots of it away.

Oprah gives money to help schools.
She even set up a school for girls in Africa.
Oprah shows us that one person can help many others.

Circle the letter for the right answer.

1. This story is MOSTLY about a _____ on TV.

   a woman   b show   c club

2. People may feel _____ after they watch Oprah's show.

   a tired   b happy   c old

3. Oprah is rich because she _____.

   a likes to read   b works hard   c helps kids

4. You can tell from the story that Oprah cares most about _____.

   a animals   b singing   c people

Write two words to finish the sentence.

Oprah uses her money to _____ _____.

What is a well?

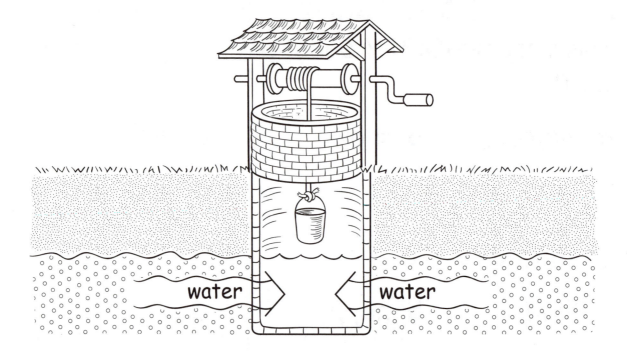

A well is a place to get water.
The water is deep in the ground.
The well is like a long tunnel.
It goes down to the water.

It is hard work to dig a well.
There must be a wall around the well.
That way no one will fall in!

It is hard work to get the water up, too.
You can use a pail with a long rope.
You drop the pail down into the water.
Then you pull it up with the rope.

Circle the letter for the right answer.

1. This story is MOSTLY about _____.

   a water b wells c pails

2. To get to the water, you must _____ a well.

   a dig b find c pull

3. At the top of a well, there is a _____ in the ground.

   a pail b rope c hole

4. People dig wells because they _____.

   a like them b need water c have rope

Write two words to finish the sentence.

Getting water from a well is _____ _____.

Who was Beatrix Potter?

Beatrix Potter lived in a tall brick house.
Beatrix liked to be in the garden.
She played with the animals there.

Soon Beatrix could tame the animals.
She took them into the house.
She named a rabbit Peter.

Beatrix liked to draw her pets.
She made up a story about each one.
She sent *The Tales of Peter Rabbit* to a child.
He loved the story!

Soon Beatrix was making lots of books.
Kids loved Peter, Flopsy, Mopsy, and Cotton-tail.
And children still read her books today.

Circle the letter for the right answer.

1. This story is MOSTLY about a _____.

    a rabbit   b girl   c book

2. Beatrix liked to _____.

    a be with animals   b sing songs

    c dig in the garden

3. In this story, to <u>tame</u> means to _____.

    a know   b hurt   c teach

4. You can tell from the story that Flopsy, Mopsy, and Cotton-tail were _____.

    a mice   b rabbits   c girls

Write two words to finish the sentence.

Beatrix Potter _____ _____ for children.

Go To Writing Page 48

WHAT ANIMAL LOOKS LIKE A LOG?

Tell how you think an alligator feels.

Writing Page

DO PEOPLE LIVE ON MARS?

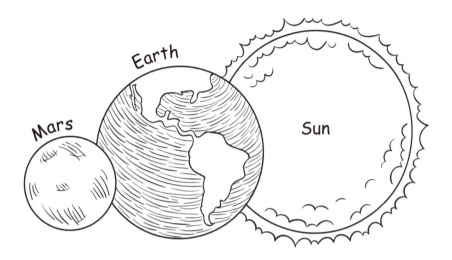

Would you like to go to Mars? Tell why or why not.

WHAT IS KARATE?

Tell about a game or sport you like.

WHY DO WE CALL SOME PEOPLE INDIANS?

Tell about the place where you live.

HOW DID ABE LINCOLN LEARN TO READ?

Tell about the book you like best.

Writing Page

WHAT DO SLED DOGS DO?

Tell about a dog you like.

WHO WAS BEATRIX POTTER?

Make up a story about a pet.